PIG JOKES AND PUZZLES

by LISA EISENBERG
and
KATY HALL

Inside illustrations by Bryan Hendrix

SCHOLASTIC INC.
New York Toronto London Auckland Sydney Tokyo

ISBN 0-590-32566

Text copyright © 1983 by Lisa Eisenberg and Katy Hall. Illustrations copyright © 1983 by Scholastic Inc. All rights reserved. Published by Scholastic Inc.

12 11 10 9 8 7 6 5 4 3 2 1   11   3 4 5 6 7/8

Printed in the U.S.A   11

In the Spotlight

Most pigs are born entertainers. They love to ham it up! Here are six pig-tures of that famous Hoggywood entertainer, Rock Gruntly. Can you find the two pig-tures that are exactly alike?

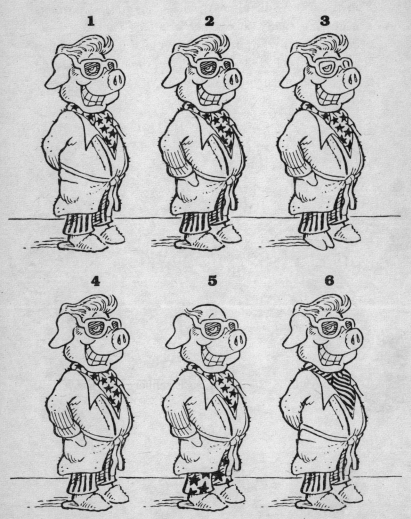

Hog Jogging

They're off! Well, almost. These jogging sweathogs are getting ready to run the annual Gruntston Marathon. But only one runner will make it to the finish line. Will it be 1, 2, 3, or 4? You can find out by jogging through the maze yourself, and may the best ham win!

Pie-in-the-Sty

All the little piggies went to market—and when they came home, they were *squealing* about all the delicious goodies they bought! Their sweet treats are listed below, and they're also in the word find grid on the opposite page. Root them out. Put a loop around each goodie as you find it. You can go up, down, forward, backward, and diagonally.

BROWNIES   COOKIES
CANDY KISSES   FUDGE
CHERRY PIE   ICE CREAM
CHOCOLATES   PUDDING
APPLE CAKE   TAFFY

What is a piglet's very favorite sweet treat?
A Pig Newton!

```
C H O C O L A T E S S I
A C A K K I E T R E C K
N N I C E C R E A M H E
D B R O W N I E S I E K
Y E R R O Y G E W C R A
K T F P U D D I N G R C
I A A C U N D U E P Y E
S T C F C D U F S P P L
S E R R F O C L A L I P
E S E Y T Y N D Y A E P
S D M S E I K O O C S A
```

Pigs' Riddle Riot

The famous comedian, Virginia Hamm, has a riddle for you: What runs all the way around a pigpen but never moves? To find out, fill in the blanks in the sentences below. The circled letters going down will reveal the answer to the riddle. (There's a word piggy bank at the bottom of the page, if you want to use it.)

1. A pig's Ⓞ __ __ __ is curly.

2. An adult pig is called a Ⓞ __ __ .

3. Groups of cows or pigs are called __ Ⓞ __ __ __ .

4. A pig's foot ends in a __ __ __ Ⓞ .

5. A baby pig is called a __ __ __ __ Ⓞ __ .

6. A pig's nose is called a __ Ⓞ __ __ __ .

7. Pigs Ⓞ __ __ __ off in hot weather by wallowing in the mud.

8. A famous book about Wilbur the pig is called *Charlotte's* __ Ⓞ __ .

herds	cool	snout	piglet
hog	tail	hoof	Web

Pig Wig Dot-to-Dot

What is a pig's favorite hairdo? To find out, start at number one and connect all the dots.

Squealers

Why did the police officer make the pig move his car?
It was in a No Porking zone!

What did the farmer say when the hog wouldn't fit
into the pen?
"There's more here than meets the sty!"

What kind of bedtime stories do piglets like best?
Pigtales!

How do pigs keep their skin so soft and smooth?
They use lots of ham lotion!

What would you get if you crossed a pig with a cat?
A sowerpuss!

Who was King Arthur's favorite knight?
   Sir Lunchalot!

Teacher: Josh, can you name five members of the hog family?

Josh: *Mother hog, father hog, and the three baby hogs?*

What is a hog's favorite musical instrument?
   The piggolo! (piccolo)

Why are pigs like tattletales?
   Because they're all squealers!

11

Piggy Mix-and-Match

When people think of a pig, they often think of a pen. And what better use for a pen than to write a saying about a pig! See if you can match the phrases on the left with the endings on the right. It won't be hard to do if you're *ham*bitious!

1. Living _____   A. piggeldy.

2. Bringing home _____   B. Pigs.

3. Higgeldy _____   C. pig in a poke.

4. Three Little _____   D. piggy went to market.

5. Never buy a _____   E. out of a sow's ear.

6. This little _____   F. stole a pig and away he run.

7. You can't make a silk purse _____   G. the bacon.

8. Tom, Tom, the piper's son, _____   H. high on the hog.

Pigs on a Blanket

Papa Boar, Mama Sow, and all the little piglets are down at the beach. Study the picture for two minutes. Then turn the page and see how much you can remember about the Swine family picnic.

Without looking back at the picture on page 13, how many of these questions can you answer?

1. How many members of the Swine family are in the picture?
2. Name the items on the beach blanket.
3. A piglet is sitting on the edge of the blanket. What is she holding? What does her T-shirt say?
4. Is Mrs. Swine wearing a bathing suit, a dress, or a T-shirt and shorts?
5. Is Mr. Swine eating a sandwich or an ice cream cone?
6. Two of the Swine children are standing on the beach. Which one is holding the beach ball?
7. Is the brother's bathing suit striped or polka-dotted?
8. Which member of the Swine family is wearing sunglasses?
9. What is Mr. Swine wearing on his head?
10. How many seagulls are on the beach?

Starstruck Maze

It all started with that glamorous Queen of the Screen, Miss Piggy. Now pigs everywhere want to leave the farm and go to Hollywood. But first they have to get out of the barnyard. Can you put them on the path to fame and fortune?

Amazo's Magic Word Squares

Amazo the Great knows that if you solve the clues and fill in the squares, the words will read the same across and down. Swine not try it?

A.

1. Porky is a famous ___.
2. Frozen water.
3. "Dinnertime! Come and ___ it!"

1	2	3
2		
3		

B.

1. Pig sound.
2. To press the wrinkles out of a shirt or dress.
3. What you smell with.
4. Past tense of know.

1	2	3	4
2			
3			
4			

C.

1. What you do at the supermarket.
2. Where bees live.
3. The chef was proud of his new microwave ——.
4. Pigs may live in or write with ——.

Pig Parts Puzzle

Go whole hog! Change just one letter in each of these words to make a part of a pig. The pigs will certainly thank you for it!

1. heed   —— —— —— ——
2. month   —— —— —— —— ——
3. feel   —— —— —— ——
4. task   —— —— —— ——
5. shout   —— —— —— —— ——
6. roof   —— —— —— ——
7. pail   —— —— —— ——
8. eats   —— —— —— ——
9. eves   —— —— —— ——
10. lets   —— —— —— ——

Pig Pen Words

Some people say pigs are boaring! But maybe you would be too if you were *pent* up in a *pen* all day. Anyway, pick up a *pen*cil and see if you can find all the words below with *pen* in them. There's no *pen*alty for missing a few! Whew!

1. What *pen* is a state?
   P E N _ _ _ _ _ _ _

2. What *pen* needs no ink?   P E N _ _ _

3. What *pen* is 1/5 of a nickel?   P E N _ _

4. What *pen* is a bird?   P E N _ _ _ _

5. What *pen* means not shut?   _ P E N

6. What *pen* would you do to
   a dull knife?   _ _ _ _ P E N

7. What *pen* do you do with money?
   _ P E N _

8. What *pen* means to occur?
   _ _ _ P E N

9. What *pen* is a five-sided shape?
   P E N _ _ _ _ _

10. What *pen* does a fireman wear to hold his
    pants up?   _ _ _ P E N _ _ _ _

Root Out the Errors

As you can see, Hamanda is hard at work taking orders at Curly's Diner. But wait! There is something wrong with this picture! See if you can root out the errors. List each one you find in the spaces below.

_____

_____

_____

_____

_____

_____

_____

_____

Hog Wit

What is a pig's favorite soft drink?
Root beer!

Why did the pig stop writing?
His pen ran out of oink!

When is a pig like a plant?
When it roots!

How is a pig's tail like getting up at sunrise?
It's twirly! (Too early!)

How do British pigs greet each other?
"Hello, old chop!"

What do pigs put on their baked potatoes?
Sower cream!

Which side of a pig has the most bristles?
The outside!

What do pigs send each other on February 14th?
Valenswines!

What are a pig's two favorite states?
New Hampshire and Pennsylvania!

What do pigs like on their hamburgers?
Piggles!

Swiney Crossword

Have you ever noticed how many pig words begin with the letter *S*? See for yourself! Fill in the answers to this porker puzzle, and you'll feel as satisfied as a sow sleeping in the sun!

ACROSS

2. A female pig (rhymes with *cow*).
3. A short nap (rhymes with *cruise*).
4. What farmers say when they want to call a pig (rhymes with *gooey*).
5. Sound a pig makes (rhymes with *short*).
7. Pigs love to eat peanut butter and jelly ____ (rhymes with *grand pitches*).
9. Past tense of sting.
10. Pigs, hogs, and boars are ____ (rhymes with *shine*).
11. A pig who's not feeling too well is feeling just so-____ (rhymes with *no*).
12. Sarah Sowerbelle's initials.

DOWN

1. A pig's cry (rhymes with *meal*).
2. The piglet brought his favorite corn cob to school for ____-and-Tell (rhymes with *glow*).
3. Food fed to pigs (rhymes with *hops*).

4. To wade through mud puddles (rhymes with *gosh*).
5. A pig's nose (rhymes with *out*).
6. A pig's home (plural).
8. Pigs' motto: "Never cry over ___ milk."
10. Pigs like all ___ of food (rhymes with *sports*).

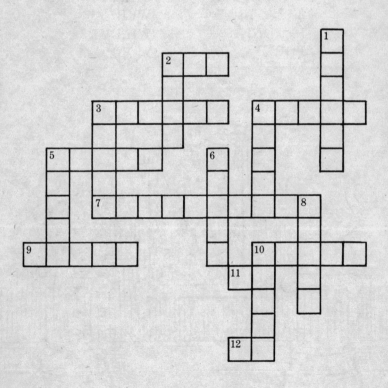

Pigs' Hall of Fame

By going up, down, backward, forward, and diagonally, see if you can search out the words that have to do with famous pigs of screen and story. Put a loop around each word as you find it.

BRICKS   STRAW
CHARLOTTE   THREE
MISS PIGGY   WEB
PETUNIA   WILBUR
PORKY   WOLF

```
P I G G P Y K R O P C
C H A R O T B I G G H
S B W E W I L B U R A
K E T E P E T U N L R
C R H E B H W O L F L
I G O R K A B U R R O
R G O H R L O T M E T
B Y F T B I C K Z E T
M I S S P I G G Y E E
M A I P E T U N I A P
```

Swine Find

Pigs are thought to be sty-at-home types, but they like the great outdoors as much as anyone! See if you can spot the ten piggies hidden in this woodland scene.

The Piggy Bank Game

This cents-able game is for two players. The game-board is on pages 32-33. The object is to get filthy rich as you go around the board. Each player uses a penny for a marker.

HOW TO START:

1. Put both markers in the Piggy Bank *START BOX*.
2. Flip another penny to decide who goes first. Take turns playing. Be sure to follow the directions on the square where you land. It's okay for two players to be on the same square.

HOW TO MOVE:

1. Each player holds up one fist.
2. Both players say together, "Piggy, piggy, piggy, BANK!"
3. On the word "BANK" each player holds up *zero*, *one*, or *two* fingers from the fist.
4. The total number of fingers that *both* players show is the number of squares the player can move.

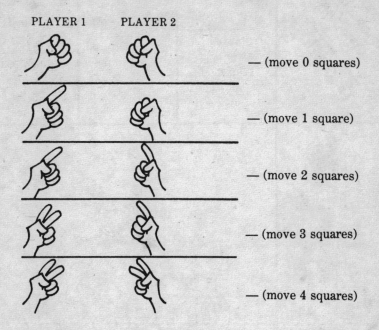

PLAYER 1   PLAYER 2

— (move 0 squares)

— (move 1 square)

— (move 2 squares)

— (move 3 squares)

— (move 4 squares)

HOW TO SCORE:
1. Each player needs a paper and pencil. Make two columns on the paper: Pennies In and Pennies Out.
2. When you land on a square where you *get* pennies, put the amount under Pennies In. When you land on a square where you *lose* pennies, put that amount under Pennies Out.
3. The game ends when one of the players (or both together) lands on Piggy Bank.
4. The players add up their Pennies In and Pennies Out columns, and then subtract Pennies Out from Pennies In. The player with the most Pennies In wins!

Just visiting; move next turn.

Hogspital

You're invited to a high sow-ciety party.

Spend 100 pennies.

You get a porking ticket. Lose 1 turn.

Free Change! Get 50 pennies.

You go hog wild at the arcade.

Shell out 100 pennies.

You convert to sow-lar energy.

Earn 150 pennies.

Stockyard market crashes.

Lose all your pennies.

Free Porking! Move next turn.

You win the Miss Hamerica contest.

Pocket 150 pennies.

You discover oil in the barnyard.

Double your pennies.

You sell your autobihography to the movies.

Earn 500 pennies.

PIGGY BANK GAME

You buy an Applecore computer.
___
Pay 200 pennies.

You win a cash prize on *Let's Make a Squeal.*
___
Gain 150 pennies.

You bet on a loin shot and win.
___
Rake in 500 pennies.

Go to the Hogspital!

Stockyard market rises.
___
Double your pennies.

You go on a shopping spree.
___
Spend 100 pennies.

You are robbed by a pig-pocket.
___
Lose 100 pennies.

You get a loin distance phone call — collect.
___
Pay 50 pennies.

You costar with Miss Piggy.
___
Earn 300 pennies.

You need a new sow-fa.
___
Pay 150 pennies.

Box

Start

Piggy Bank

Hamhock's Secret Sign-off

Famous detective Hamhock Holmes has written a letter to Miss Piggy asking her to dinner. Although Hamhock is a super swine sleuth, he's very shy. In fact, he's hidden the letter's sign-off inside a puzzle! You can discover how he ended his letter by crossing out the boxes containing Q, X, Y, and Z.

W	X	I	Y	Z	T	Q
X	H	Z	H	Y	X	O
G	S	Q	A	X	N	Z
Y	X	D	Q	K	Z	I
S	Y	S	Z	E	Q	S

_____ _____ ___ _____,

Hamhock Holmes

Hig Pigs

A *hig pig* is a riddle in which the answer is two rhyming words of one syllable. Example: What is a large hog? A *big pig*. See if you can guess the answers to these hig pigs.

1. What is a hog's hairpiece?

   a P ___ ___   W ___ ___

2. What is a loud male pig's growl?

   a B ___ ___ ___   R ___ ___ ___

3. What do you call a group of pigs waiting to get into the movies?

   a S ___ ___ ___ ___   L ___ ___ ___

4. What is a sound made by a very small pig?

   a R ___ ___ ___   G ___ ___ ___ ___

5. What kind of eating utensil is used by a pig?

   a P ___ ___ ___   F ___ ___ ___

6. What is a hog's favorite kind of dance?

   a P ___ ___   J ___ ___ ___

Pig-ture Rebus

When is a pig like ink? To find the answer, simply solve this piggy pig-ture rebus.

1.

W + _____ ____

2.

-kn ___

3.

-k,-s ___

4.

-P ___

5.

___

6.

-ny ____

More Hog Wit

What goes "knio, knio"?
A pig talking backward!

What position does a pig play in football?
Loinbacker!

How does a pig feel when he can't talk?
Disgruntled!

How did the farmer feel when he got stuck in the pigpen?
Sty-mied!

Why do pigs make such great sports fans?
They're always rooting?

Hair-y Word Hunt

Did you know that at least 50 words can be made from
the letters in the word, **bristles**? Write all the words
you can think of in the corncobs on these pages. Don't
feel hog-tied if you can't get all 50—25 is still terrific!

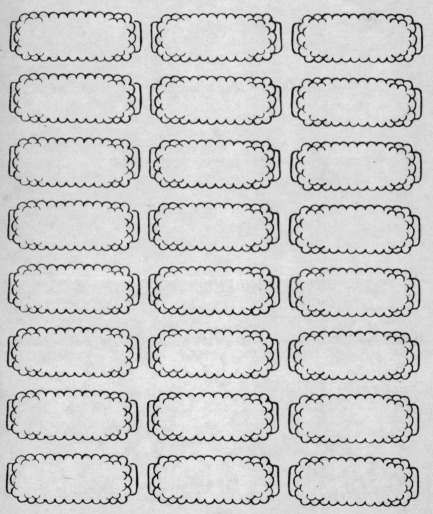

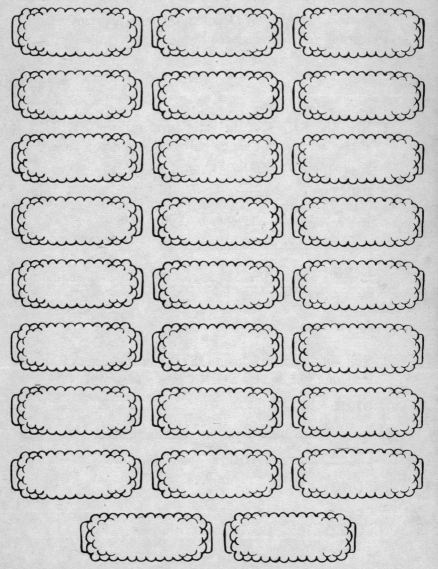

Hog Ladders

If you can do these word ladders, the fairy hog-mother will grunt you three wishes!

1. Help the RUNT of the litter turn into the KING of the barnyard. Change only one letter at a time to make a new word.

   RUNT

   ___ ___ ___ ___ I have ___ the doorbell.

   ___ ___ ___ ___ Telephone noise.

   KING

2. Help a musical sow get to the top of the charts by changing her squeaky OINK into a sweet SONG.

   OINK

   ___ ___ ___ ___ Basin for washing dishes.

   ___ ___ ___ ___ What a singer does.

   SONG

3. Help change a baby PIG into a grown-up SOW.

PIG

— — — Opposite of little.

— — — Swamp or marsh (rhymes with *fog*).

— — — Half of a dog's bark; __-wow.

SOW

4. Finally, help the new pig on the block get settled by changing the BARN into home, sweet HOME.

BARN

— — — — Without shoes or socks; __ foot.

— — — — Sound-alike word for boar.

— — — — Aching or painful.

— — — — "I'd like __ more, please."
(Rhymes with *come*.)

HOME

Pigs' Super Crossword

ACROSS

1. Baby pig.
5. Chick talk (rhymes with *deep*).
8. Doctor (abbrev.).
9. Do, re, ___, fa....
10. Georgia (abbrev.).
12. General Motors (abbrev.).
14. Ophelia Ivy Hogg (initials).
16. Opposite of he.
17. Yukon Territory (abbrev.).
18. "On your mark, ___ set, *go!*"
19. Opposite of hard (rhymes with *breezy*).
20. Home, sweet home to a hog.
21. Hard-working pigs deserve a ___ on the back from time to time.
22. Alboart's nickname.
24. South America (abbrev.).

25. "This little ___ went to market ..." (plural).
27. Lois Lane (initials).
28. Not the beginning, but the ___.
29. Okay (abbrev.).

DOWN

1. Pig-shaped object that holds money.
2. Opposite of come.
3. Nickname for Edward.
4. "If at first you don't succeed, ___ again."
5. This pig word means very stubborn.
6. Dorothy's aunt in the *Oz* stories.
7. This pig word is a kind of ride.

1		2		3	4		5		6	7
				8					9	
10			11				12	13		
		14		15		16				
17			18				19			
		20				21				
22					23				24	
		25				26				
		27			28				29	

11. Pig word for a braid of hair.

13. Veal, beef, or pork.

15. Sound-alike word for hay.

23. How old you are.

25. Party line (abbrev.).

26. Not out.

43

Pork Avenue Maze

Hurry, hurry, hurry! There's a big sale on at the Pork Avenue Jewelry Store. Piggy Sue, the beauty of the barnyard, wants to get there early to check out the bargains. Can you find her <u>shortcut</u> through the maze?

Runty Crostic

When is a runt *not* a runt? When you find the answer to this riddle, you'll *squeal* with laughter! Solve the clues and fill in the blanks. Then transfer the letters to the same numbered boxes in the grid on the opposite page. All the pigs are rooting for you on this one!

A. What insects buzz around the picnic table?

$\overline{}\ \overline{}\ \overline{}\ \overline{}\ \overline{}$
23 22 5   3   11

B. The runt grew so fast, its new clothes didn't

$\overline{}\ \overline{}\ \overline{}$ anymore.
17 14 19

C. The piglet wasn't very tall. She only came up to

my $\overline{}\ \overline{}\ \overline{}\ \overline{}$ (rhymes with *bee*).
9   4   10 21

D. A boar who has gone bald might wear a

$\overline{}\ \overline{}\ \overline{}$.
1   18 15

E. 2 sows plus 2 sows equals 4 sows. This is a

$\overline{}\ \overline{}\ \overline{}\ \overline{}$ problem (rhymes with *bath*).
7   12 6   2

F. After the mud-wrestling match, all the pigs washed

up with plenty of $\overline{}\ \overline{}\ \overline{}\ \overline{}$ and water.
20 16 8   13

| 1 | 2 | 3 | 4 | | 5 | 6 | | 7 | 8 | 9 | 10 | 11 | | 12 |
| 13 | 14 | 15 | | 16 | 17 | | 18 | 19 | 20 | 21 | 22 | 23 | ! | |

Pigs' Spell-Down

If you solve the clues and fill in the grid, you'll be tickled pink! That's because the circled letters will reveal the answer to this riddle: What do pigs like to eat with their sandwiches?

1. Another word for root.
2. How you drink from a straw.
3. Another word for friend or buddy.
4. One of Santa's helpers.
5. Sound a punctured balloon makes.
6. Opposite of lose.
7. Opposite of little.
8. Griselda Gloria Grunt's initials.
9. Opposite of high.
10. Not him.
11. A call for help.

Diamonds in the Trough

This is a real jewel of a puzzle. Use the clues to complete these word diamonds. When you're finished, you'll see that the answers read the same across and down.

1. This letter is in *swine* but not in *whine*.
2. Past tense of see.
3. Lettuce is usually used to make this.
4. Dogs' tails do this.
5. This letter is in *mud* but not in *smug*.

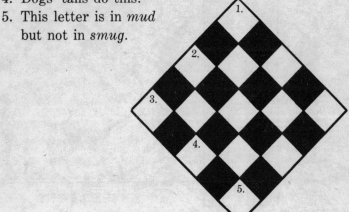

1. This letter is in *snort* but not in *north*.
2. A pigpen.
3. A high-spirited horse (rhymes with *deed*).
4. Opposite of no.
5. This letter is in *dinner* but not in *thinner*.

1. This letter is in *squeal* but not in *square*.
2. What this book is all about (singular).
3. Road hogs often go over the speed ____.
4. ____ rummy is a favorite piggy card game.
5. The last letter is in *piglet* but not in *glimpse*.

Ham Rock Puzzle

The Road Hogs, that ever-popular singing group, is back in town to give a concert. Below are the names of each of the band members. See if you can fit each name into the grid on the opposite page.

BOARIS	PINKY
CURLY	STOUT
HAMMY	SQUEALER
HOOFER	TUSKER

Cross-Number Puzzle

If you can fill in the hog's share of answers in this puzzle, you'll win the Albert Swinestein award!

ACROSS

1. How many pigs have 25 tails?
3. Number of pigs in the famous story plus 100.
5. If a boar has 512 bristles, and 6 fall out, how many are left?
6. Age of a sow who has lived for 6 decades plus 4 years.
7. Piggy Sue is now 11 years old. How old will she be on her next birthday?
8. Number of days in 2 weeks plus 1 day.
9. 11 little piggies dancing with a hen; 1 fainted from the heat, and then there were ___.
10. 50 piglets have ___ feet.
11. Number of years in 5 centuries plus 55.
12. Miss Piggy just got a $70-a-week raise. She was earning $600 a week. How much is she earning now?
15. Porklet is saving boxtops from her favorite cereal. If she gets 2 more, she'll have 30. How many boxtops does she have now?
16. 1984 + 2 years.
17. If a piglet can eat 150 apple cores in a week, how many can it eat in 2 weeks?
18. 10 runts + 10 sows + 10 boars + 9 piglets = ___.
19. Comes after 255.

DOWN

2. Half of 1104 house-sows are getting wall-to-wall carpeting. How many sows is that?

3. 5 grunts **+** 4 oinks **+** 7 snorts = ___.

4. If the Road Hogs gave a concert every day for a year, how many days would that be?

7. 50 piglets have ___ ears.

8. The Hog Census Report shows that 100 new pigs moved to Bristleton, a town of 950. What is the town's population now?

9. 125 sows entered a Miss Piggy look-alike contest. All but 4 won. How many sows were the winners?

11. Number of pigs in the rhyme, "This little piggy . . ." plus 52.

12. 2666 backward.

13. Pen State wrestling champ Brutus Hogg once weighed in at 450 pounds. He's gained 30 pounds. How much does he weigh now?

14. 500 pigs minus 1 pig equals ___ pigs.

15. Number of this clue plus 5.

16. People as well as pigs consider this to be an unlucky number.

17. Three football teams of 12 players each = ___ pigskin players.

55

Sty-lish Words Workout

Each word below contains the word, *sty*. To complete each word, solve the clues and fill in the blanks. This puzzle shouldn't make you squeal — there's a word piggy bank at the bottom, if you get stuck. Grab your tru*sty* pencil and don't be too ha*sty*!

1. How you feel when you need something to drink.   ___ ___ ___ ___ sty

2. This word means unkind, unpleasant, or spiteful.   ___ ___ sty

3. Another word for foggy.   ___ ___ sty

4. Your bike might get this way if it's left out in the rain.   ___ ___ sty

5. "___ the Snowman."   ___ ___ ___ sty

6. Covered with powder or soot.   ___ ___ sty

7. Another word for delicious.   ___ ___ sty

8. "Your ___." (What you might call a king or a queen.)   ___ ___ ___ ___ sty

thirsty	misty	Frosty	tasty
nasty	rusty	dusty	majesty

56

Grunts 'n' Grins

What did the pig say when its brother fell into the meatgrinder?

"I never sausage a thing!"

Which two pigs sang a duet?

A sowprano and a boaratone!

What soup does a pig like best?

Boarscht!

How does a pig feel after he's eaten dinner?

Slop-happy!

What's a pig's favorite ballet?

Swine Lake!

Answers

p. 3 **In the Spotlight**
2 and 4

pp. 4-5 **Hog Jogging**

pp. 6-7 **Pie-in-the-Sty**

p. 8 **Pigs' Riddle Riot**
1. tail; 2. hog; 3. herds; 4. hoof; 5. piglet;
6. snout; 7. cool; 8. Web.

p. 9 **Pig Wig Dot-to-Dot**

p. 12 **Piggy Mix-and-Match**
1. H; 2. G; 3. A; 4. B; 5. C; 6. D; 7. E; 8. F.

p. 15 **Starstruck Maze**

¹P	²I	³G
²I	C	E
³G	E	T

¹O	²I	³N	⁴K
²I	R	O	N
³N	O	S	E
⁴K	N	E	W

¹S	²H	³O	⁴P
²H	I	V	E
³O	V	E	N
⁴P	E	N	S

p. 18　　**Pig Parts Puzzle**
1. head; 2. mouth; 3. feet; 4. tusk; 5. snout;
6. hoof; 7. tail; 8. ears; 9. eyes; 10. legs.

p. 19　　**Pig Pen Words**
1. Pennsylvania; 2. pencil; 3. penny; 4. penguin;
5. open; 6. sharpen; 7. spend; 8. happen; 9. pentagon; 10. suspenders.

pp. 20-21　**Root Out the Errors**
The "R" is backward on the menu that says "Curly's Diner."
One of the chairs has pig legs instead of real ones.
One pig is about to eat another pig's tie in a bun.
One pig is getting ready to eat a flower pot instead of some food on a plate.
On the clock on the wall, there are two "3's."
The calendar on the wall is upside down.
One pig's place is set with a knife, a fork, and a wrench.
On Hamanda's tray, there is a live fish in a bun.

p. 24-25   **Swiney Crossword**

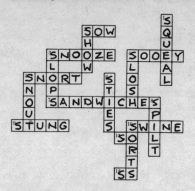

pp. 26-27   **Pigs' Hall of Fame**

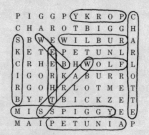

pp. 28-29   **Swine Find**

61

p. 34   **Hamhock's Secret Sign-off**
With hogs and kisses

p. 35   **Hig Pigs**
1. Pig Wig; 2. Boar Roar; 3. Swine Line; 4. Runt
Grunt; 5. Pork Fork; 6. Pig Jig.

p. 36   **Pig-ture Rebus**
When it is in a pen.

pp. 38-39   **Hair-y Word Hunt**

I	its	bite	site	lies
be	let	bier	tier	Bess
is	set	best	tile	bless
it	sit	list	stir	bliss
ire	bet	lest	rest	stile
tie	tis	isle	rise	tribe
lie	lit	less	bile	tries
sis	bit	sire	Tess	tress
rib	belt	slit	rile	sties
sir	Bert	silt	tire	sister

pp. 40-41   **Hog Ladders**

1. RUNT	2. OINK	3. PIG	4. BARN
rung	sink	big	bare
ring	sing	bog	bore
KING	SONG	bow	sore
		SOW	some
			HOME

pp. 42-43   **Pigs' Super Crossword**

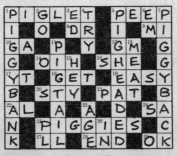

pp. 44-45 **Pork Avenue Maze**

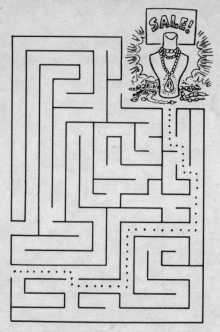

pp. 46-47 **Runty Crostic**

A. flies; B. fit; C. knee; D. wig; E. math; F. soap.

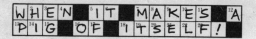

pp. 48-49 **Pigs' Spell-Down**

pp. 50-51 Diamonds in the Trough

pp. 52-53 Ham Rock Puzzle

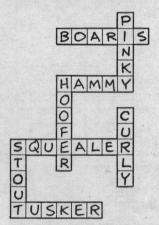

pp. 54-55 Cross-Number Puzzle

p. 56 Sty-lish Words Workout

1. thirsty; 2. nasty; 3. misty; 4. rusty; 5. Frosty;
6. dusty; 7. tasty; 8. majesty.